BRAIDED [UN]BE-LONGING

Braided [Un]Be-Longing

ISBN-13: 979-8-9877417-1-9

Library of Congress Control Number: 2023902802

All inquiries and requests should be addressed to the author:
www.rosannaalvarez.com

Cover art and illustrations by Rosanna Alvarez

Set in Minion Variable Concept

First US Edition 2023

Published by Ocote Libre Press
in the United States of America.
www.ocotelibrepress.com

BRAIDED [UN]BE-LONGING

ROSANNA ALVAREZ

OCOTE LIBRE PRESS

Para mis tres guerreras,

and to the little girl who waited
patiently through the longing

"Poetry is not only dream and vision; it is the skeleton architecture of our lives. It lays the foundations of change, a bridge across our fears of what has never been before."

- Audre Lorde

"Rise. All of you rise to speak your truth. We need more people who name themselves after the land, instead of naming the land after themselves."

- Lyla June

"we cede nothing.
forget nothing. the
voices are here. the voices are with
us. within us.

the voices do not end. the singing
does not end."

- ire'ne lara silva

FOREWORD | by Brenda Vaca

According to my word sister Rosanna Alvarez - hermana de la pluma, fellow creator of in tlili in tlapali, in the red of the blood and the black of the soil - this book has been incubating forever.

When she says forever, she means forever. In *Braided [Un]Be-Longing*, Rosanna Alvarez resounds the singing bowl, the drum and heartbeat of Turtle Island, and calls in our ancestors and ourselves, all in the same breath. She has told me before, "We've always been having this conversation." But, I did not understand what she meant until now.

I first met Rosanna Alvarez through a wonderful non-profit organization in Eastside San José, California called Somos Mayfair. I was an ordained reverend at the time, and Rosanna worked diligently in the Mayfair neighborhood, otherwise known as Sal Si Puedes - the same Eastside barrio that raised and reared labor organizer Cesar Chavez. Our organizations shared space and a parking lot. Somos rented out the old church's La Trinidad Fellowship Hall and reached young local families looking to organize, nourish, and advocate for their own well-being in all its senses. At the time, they had an emphasis on improving the literacy rate in the K-3rd grade community. This was indeed an uphill climb in the shadow of the technological Goliath that is the Silicon Valley where rent is continually skyrocketing, especially in the wake of the great recession of 2008. The neighborhood was gutted by the real estate market crash and boasted the most foreclosures in the U.S. at the time, due to predatory lending practices.

One afternoon, Rosanna and I met for coffee at the local Starbucks on Story and King. Somehow, and I don't know how, the subject of writing and poetry came up. It was inevitable - dos Xicanas hociconas (as la Poeta Rosanna would say) were bound to bring up their love language when talking about our dreams and hopes for the future. The griot spirit surged as we sat down that afternoon.

At the time, I was a closet poet. Weekly sermons - in English y Español - took up much of my time. But every now and then a poem would sneak in, making it's way into my notebooks and phone memos. Dreams of crafting a book and lancing it into the world were a distant longing. What I remember I took away from that fateful conversation with Rosanna Alvarez was a reignited spark to engage in the ancient practice of storytelling: in xochitl in cuicatl.

Fast forward about ten years later and I have the honor to write this foreword for her long-awaited debut collection *Braided [Un]Be-Longing*. And it is, indeed, una trensa fuerte that intertwines the complexities of identity, spirituality, and the ache and beauty of the human experience.

In her preface she entitled "The Journey," Alvarez mentions that she believes books find their way to us, and she is right. As I began to make my way through this collection, my eyes welled up with tears on several occasions as they might during a long-awaited reunion. Remember that person you hadn't seen for a long time? And then you found yourselves with one another so happy to share presence and a hug? Rosanna awoke that amor en mi.

There is something resuscitative about this body of work that the Poet reminds us is flor y canto. Indeed, it is "a collective excavation," as Alvarez writes. It is uncomfortable and painful, yet mostly, it is a suspiro - a sigh of relief to finally belong, be seen, beheld, and assured page after page that it is quite enough to simply be. It is enough.

La tinta negra y la tinta roja de los codices are harkened here. The red of the cochinilla chupando los nopales. El negro de la tierra después de una lluvia profunda, verde y fructífera. Muddy mineral mayhem just everywhere. Y allí viene la artista. La quien busca la luz - oh, yes, this Xicana searched for the light and found it.

These poems will call out the poetry in you. The title alone is like a mathematical equation, daring the reader to go back and remember an ancient knowing to which we belong:

> *The ancestors -they say we don't have to struggle to learn;*
> *It's about how we learn to remember*
>
> - from "I Dream"

Arriving to just beyond the center of the collection was like climbing a mountain to its apex. Back-to-back poems from "Just People"; "cae mal, caiman"; onward to "Unceremonious Mitote" and "They Mean," pack an unapologetic punch rife with sacred rage:

> *Our land was never for sale,*
> *and our muertos are not for the taking.*
>
> > - from "cae mal, caiman"

> *her native [Spanish colonizer] tongue*
> > - from "They Mean"

> *Lost track of the dispossessed native lands*
> *back when*
> *they were boarding up babies*
> *to kill the Indian and save the man*
> > - from "They Mean"

> *and our rage*
> *doesn't know*
> *where*
> *to begin*

> *so, I write poems*
> > - from "Strategic All(lies)"

I found "Unceremonious Mitote" to be the center of the nugget in this fine collection. A navel so stanky it puts novelas to shame. A hard confrontation - because does a mujer always have to support other mujeres? What of the ones who corrupt and "strike first"? Damn, the poet really put the question like a dagger to my heart. When have I been this woman? When have I allowed such a woman to defile my presence? Oh, yes, we must acknowledge, sometimes we women are part of the problem. The word "unceremonious" is used back to back - strikingly so - when ceremony and the sacred is everything to the poet.

Alvarez reminds us that our trensas are our resistance and our connection to our ancestral ways. This collection crescendoes at perhaps my favorite poem "I Dream." Although, I must say, it is very difficult to choose just one favorite. It is true, this collection is braided together in such a way that makes you look at each strand, up close, each pelito essential and accounted for, but then, equally important to pause and step back. Behold the whole in its essence. I saw the braids of this collection in its order and form. I peeked the braid over the year when the Poet would share tidbits on her social media pages. I heard the bees and the colibris trilling that a time of birth was at hand. I felt the longing of the storyteller pouring out the heart of her desire. Oh, yes, Poet. It is enough, you are simply more than enough in your being.

Alvarez's collection joins the growing pantheon of lyrical medicine during this poetic renaissance. "[P]oetry is dead," the New York Times published in an op-ed. piece at the end of 2022. Shared by fellow poet, James Coats, after a community reading where hella poets showed up to drop gems, it was as jarring to hear as "God is dead." But, in my humble opinion, NYT, you're dead-wrong. In fact, it is the dead come back to life - an astounding resurrection of our ancestors and life-affirming practice of storytelling. It is, in fact, storytelling's oldest form: the oral storytelling impulse that graces hearth and home in and beyond Turtle Island. It is a ceremony that has kept our vital power alive over what was an otherwise desecrating time in human history by the hands of the church and state. Alvarez, in xochitl in cuicatl, invites the reader into this ceremony. It is up to you to allow it to be enough.

As I neared the end of the collection, la trensa se convirtió en un río. I got a sense that I was, in fact, flowing on a river. Some lines hard stones, still others were pebbles that massaged rather than injured. Una sobadora con sus letras. The river's flow had been carrying me downstream all along. Because I trust this poet - this sister of the plume - this wielding wordsmith with the harsh machete of two colonizer tongues and the emerging indigenous one like fresh water spring. Oh, I am alive, and I am reminded and urged:

> *The revolution takes a stance, demanding that I . . .*
> *Don't walk. Dance.*
> -from "Drum Speak"

Alvarez takes the reader by the hand and shows them a world to which we have always belonged.

Thank you, Poeta, for being so intentional in gestating this work of art in word and in visual form with strategically placed inked art.

You, oh artist, are one we have all been waiting for.

Tlazocamati.

c/s Brenda Vaca

ACKNOWLEDGEMENTS

I am forever grateful to the constellation of folks who have shaped me in this braided journey:

My kids, for being constant creativity collaborators, spirited adventurers, your fire inspires me. Beyond being your mother, you have taught me so much about what it means to be givers of life.

The Mr., for believing in my words and for learning to like red wine just enough to come along and hold my purse while I am on stage.

My parents, for instilling in me a love of reading and for indulging my sense of imagination. I know you did your best and it is more than enough.

My sisters, for keeping my kids busy and for being the first people outside of our parents who thought the world of me when we were kids. I hope you feel the retroactive apapacho of my words.

My brothers whose fumblings have provided so much poetic inspiration (ha!) and for surviving my first-born accidental co-parenting ways.

The tías who allowed me a seat at the Lotería table, even as a kid.

The tíos who reminded me of the gentleness and humor of men.

Dolores Avila for being the creatrix co-conspirator, always reminding me about the wisdom and grounding powers of trees and for passing along the wise mantra of your papa.

Las Andariegas for growing from collaborating colegas to friends, comadres and sisters. Ana Lilia Soto for constantly being on the line, whether it be by phone, online, or making the drive. Marlene Chavez for the years of friendship, carcajadas, and for teaching us the sharp-shooting ways of our legacy as mujeres de la revolución.

The Kalpulli Izkalli camaradas, including Carla Torres and Yolanda Castro, for the fierce collective determination you carry and for holding a space where we can remember our cultura and center our communities.

Brenda Vaca and Elodia Esperanza Benitez for taking the plunge that I perpetually interpret as a nudge and for affirming time and time again the layers of why and how we do this work.

To the beautiful humans in this journey: Mia X. Hernandez for braiding this señora into your mix. Apryl Berney for the virtual hype sessions and for believing in my writing dreams. Carla Collins, Tamara Alvarado, and Rebeca Burciaga for your constant support and for showing me what it truly means to show up relentlessly with heart in the work you do. Teresa Castellanos for reminding us of the power of a good apapacho. Donna Castañeda, Norma Salas, and Marisol Escalera for all the years of friendship - you're all family now.

The students who have enabled my poetry and helped it emerge from my chicken-scratch indecipherable journals to the mic and now to the tangible collection here.

The Chicana and Chicano Studies Department and El Centro at San José State University for welcoming my full (and fool) self and for the poetic encouragement throughout the years.

My elders and fellow board members of La Raza Historical Society of Santa Clara Valley for the commitment and the cariño you put into maintaining a collective archive of our gente.

The team of Eastside Magazine for trusting me with our stories that run parallel to my poetry. It all started with the Multicultural Arts Leadership Institute. The experience has truly reminded me of who we are and who we come from as a community of story-makers and storytellers.

My teachers throughout my years of East San José schooling and to the profes at Santa Clara University and San José State who affirmed and encouraged my love of stories and writing.

The Poetess Kalamu Chaché for inviting poets to play on the air-waves and for modeling love and light in a myriad of poetic ways.

To my communities at large for the love and fire, danza and heart; it is a beautiful kind of chaos sometimes.

To you, Dear Reader, for coming across these words and braiding your journey with countless others.

There will be more.

BRAIDED [UN]BE-LONGING

ROSANNA ALVAREZ

CONTENTS

THE JOURNEY

We tend to think we come upon and find books by our own process of selection and choosing, and yet, there is a part of me that believes books find their way to us. The book you hold in your hands invites you to journey with me as I re-collect beyond resilience to that space of legacy, history, power, humanity, and existence. This work is a result of several years of being in poetic conversation with myself, while sharing that journey with a variety of audiences online and in person; via social media; over the airwaves; and on the microphone with audiences large and small -always with the aim of reminding ourselves of our place past the longing, that space where simply being is enough.

In coming to a space of feeling more and more compelled to share the poems as a collection, I've come to remember that this is a journey that also reflects a process of collective excavation. The poems call on us to remember the legacy of flor y canto as part of a grounded history that speaks through sincerity; where the truth of our hearts is shared on display.

The poems are intentionally braided in a way that weaves us into conversation across space and time. While I have been deeply intentional about how I've represented them here,

1

this collection is, in large part, a reflection of how the poems have disrupted my sense of linear time throughout the years. As the words found their way to me, beckoning me to write them down, I often found myself circling back to remind myself of the hope, strength, and cariño past that space of exclusion and belonging to the power of *simply being*. In revisiting my own words through the years and feeling their affirmation in the face of struggle, the mix of thorns and tenderness is offered here as a glimpse into how I have found myself going back to them, letting them speak in the context of whatever it is I am grappling with. Sometimes their meaning shifts, sometimes the poems both challenge and affirm, and other times, the poems inspire an entire other layer of poems that talk back.

If you came across this book as someone who identifies as an ally, and feel a bit of a sting with the sweetness here, push through it, stay for a while, and think about how you can do better, because the truth is we can all do better to be better. These words are my efforts to offer some sweet with the bitter and build from that space of honesty, sincerity, and harmony that is more of a dance where stumbling is necessary.

c/s Rosanna Alvarez

The Willow Tree Re-members

para que queremos la mesa
si somos de la tierra

Backwards from today, we danced around a willow tree, rooted as relatives of this land. Subversive gatherings of grounded ceremony under a crescent moon. An orange tractor disrupting the crisp air relocating rough dried wood over a bed of dried eucalyptus. Tending fire. Spirit offering wisdom. Greeting nopales with blessings of romero bearing witness. To healing songs channeled across space and time. Cycling in circles. Robust. Highway back to passage. Weaving, braiding, being past the longing toward belonging past a colonized confining set to rhyme.

Movement. Repeat. Remembrance. Dance.

Obligation Emancipation
AN HOCICONA PROCLAMATION

Out of obligation, I allowed myself to be forced into silence. I participated in the silence knowing full well I had no responsibility, or accountability, in the tragedies themselves. I find myself thinking about writing and beautiful prose comes to me. It is poetic. It is lovely. It is painful. It is my truth. At the same time, I know that my truth exposes the glass house of lies that others have built and where they comfortably reside. Even now, with my pen to the paper, I hesitate to delve into the unpacking of my truth because obligation tugs at my sense of doubt and is intricately entangled with every lesson handed down about love. Therein lies the dilemma –ripping off the bandages that cover my wounds requires a betrayal. Speaking my full truth disregards the (sigh) façade that has served others so well. But, I have to weigh that against my self-betrayal, and while my willingness to "speak" and my need to shout my truth is ironically tied to obligation, I find that I am less torn.

Out of obligation to my daughters and the generations that follow me, I break the silence in hopes that I will break the cycle. I embrace the healing and release you. Old friend, you have served me well, protecting me in a hard shell transformed into a form of resilience as I grew into a space where I could embrace the softness from a place of pure love.

Contemplating, torn, self-imposed torture while waiting to exhale. I've lived most of my life as if that expression were the guiding force of my existence. Well, I'm done waiting. In coming to my own journey of self-awareness, self-consciousness, self-fulfillment, I shift my footing and emancipate myself from what I have allowed to hold me back. Replacing fear with love and compassion, I shout my truth through these written words. I declare power over my own destiny and while it is informed by my past, it is defined by my perception and intention.

I find the courage to release myself from so many things.

"Are you ready?" I hear that little voice of self-doubt invading my jaguar sense of bravery, attempting to tame the wild horse that drives my soul. With a long and heavy breath, I respond, "Do we ever really know?" In the habit of meeting a question with a question, I find that ounce of courage I need to truly take the leap. In we go, and to go in, we must go back. In time. For on this journey, I must face that girl –the child who kept the faith that one day I would come, take her by the hand, and love her unconditionally.

Be. Longing

And how are the children
of a literate people
-- systemically vandalized
whose histories are regal?

who sometimes lack words
so far beyond feeble,
their hearts rule their minds
they're serpent and eagle

sensing wise truths
respecting the land,
they are poem and dance
intellect in their hands

nurture them whole
speaking beauty to power,
seeds in their veins
canto hondo full flowers

                --in xochitl in cuicatl

Ocote

My medicine has always come from books;
books have always been medicine.

They told us we came from an oral culture, incapable of writing and archiving our stories; that we leaned toward folkloric expressions by way of artesanía; presented to us like an "or" and an "and then" rather than a quite simply "is" and "has always been" along with the perpetual bridging of the "and" --

Later I learned they burned our books upon arrival;
and I thought about how they burned women too . . .

Healing Reflections

I find comfort in staring at this face –my face. Some mistaken it for vanity, and to some degree, maybe it is. Yet, this is the face that I run to for solace. I find strength in that reflection –a reflection of centuries of lives before me; the combined result of thousands of decisions leading to my existence into this world and in this life. Perhaps one of my ancestors wore this face in another time and found comfort in the same reflection. Maybe I resided in these eyes in a previous life, having stared out at the sea of faces who looked on as they projected their desires, fears, and contradictions as they burned the accused; her only transgressions refusing to cede her magic. A feral inclination to maintain the integrity of her essence as a way of honoring the grandmother's before her. As I stare at my reflection, the face staring back offers centuries of resilience, secrets of lives unwritten, and the poetry of the unspoken. This face has worn and held my joys, my fears, my sadness, transforming through time as my eyes–hopeful and fierce–still hold on to that fire as I reclaim my magic, refusing to apologize for the healing of my soul.

Antes. de mí

They work so hard
aggressively exclusively
to remind me
I am nobody
not understanding
that is
precisely
who
I long to be

Nobody

Just a person

still
worthy
of dignity

semillas

They say springtime brings renewal
times of life, warmth, joy, and flows
and as the days surely get longer
my introspection grows

                      And I ponder beyond wonder . . .

About so much said unspoken
of continual expectations shrouded in negotiation
prone elation prolongation
Injudicious moderation.

                      And I ponder beyond wonder . . .

How the grounded and the strong
unleash a dignity in grief
in the scheme of this motif
that is said does not belong

                      And I wonder beyond ponder . . .

How the rooted hold each other
call on tears that have been swallowed
summon them with veneration
sacred screams of transformation

                      -- when they've been buried for so long.

Palabras Floridas

I pad my language with flowery words,
Or so the accusation goes.
An attempt at forced submission,
When rage courses through unworthy foes.

My response: anything but silent.
Ocelotl, the jaguar, cunning
Skilled, observing, unrelenting
The aftermath of words, just stunning.

My consciousness refusing
to commingle with the venom
poisonous weeds, smoking mirrors,
non-disguising, forcing healing
through just seeds.

Stubborn, jaw-clenched, indignation,
Using words. Obliteration.
History. Heritage. Preservation.
Beginning. Ending. Reiteration.

Palabras floridas. Through the haze.
Antepasados. Reconnecting.
Own the phrase.
Love Self, reflecting.

These flowery words, I am embracing.

Jardín de Flores

Day 1:

> *a Huitzilopochtli yo le doy mis flores*

From birth, we are primed
To be in a constant state of war
Coded litmus test of belonging
Taught to always long for more

Day 2:

> *a Huitzilopochtli le doy mis amores*

Socialized to battle ourselves daily
Expunging the grandeur of our core
Complicitly blind to our inherent sovereignty
Dismissing the power of folklore

Day 3:

a Huitzilopochtli yo le doy mis flores

Excavating traumas beyond reservation
Resettling the bounds of the ground floor
Holding ourselves in preservation
Discarding all pretense in order to soar

Day 4:

a Huitzilopochtli le doy mis amores

Recalibrated recollections of remembrance
Reconciling wholeness, as we pour
In atonement of spirited legacies
Worth relentlessly fighting for.

Landed Migration

Drawn to the backwoods
of the Mississippi sky
Consumed by
Breathtaking Clouds
in full glory
opulence surrounds

Heirs of racist histories
Displaced tension
Wondering what if . . .

Had her foremothers traveled

                          . . . east
          . . . instead of . . .
west . . .

                 gathering home

                 Feeling the pull
                unknown calling
          Lushness of magnolia bloom

                      Lands

For decades learned
"Not welcome here"
the subtle rush
Beckoning
to abandon
pretense.

See
Myself
Under that sky
Barefoot

Moist earth peaking
through exposed toes

Prop her home on stilts
Just to feel that
Absorbing arid stillness

Where bittersweet
Sweet tea, hot taters
Pink bougainvilleas
Shrubbed of green
Trains
Roar past
Murky muddled waters
Clearer than
Baptismal lakes

Gripping hearts
Through
confederate magpies

Swayed

silent joys
of whispered withers
soulful trees
spotted with
diagonal crosses
signifying
crushed crux
treasured dreams
colonel-claimed
souls

imprinted echo
of ripping seams
antiquities of homes
recalling

residual echoes
of those
whose stilts were weakened
buckled at the knees
sagging rolling slowly
disappearing back
into those embossed lands

welcomed by the sweet smell
of luscious green
enveloping enshrouding
bearing witness with the cicadas
reaching out

as she lifts each foot back
into her tin box
on wheels

carrying speckled traces of lost
longing

back out
to the open
road searching
further east

uncovering recovery

laced with dreams untold

               with/in lands of un/be-longing.

Scarred Battlegrounds

They have this newly implemented "community building" thing at the kids' school where they stay out on the blacktop and do the whole Pledge of Allegiance and sing "This Land is Your Land" and I'm feeling the full force of all the contradictions in the context of where this is happening, and I can't quite find the words to capture how spiritually damaging this feels as an extension of the fictional narrative it all represents – a narrative that exists under the façade of diversity & inclusion in a land founded on violence and exclusion. The subtlety of the closing – "this land was made for you and me"—somehow equally imposing, feels like a not so subtle indoctrination – a nod to the idea that this land is ours to exploit.

Seemingly harmless activities cut deep when I'm trying to teach my guerreras that we belong to the land, as I am faced with the daily reality of having to reinforce their humanity, struggling as best as I can to teach them how to demand to be seen and heard in the fullness of that humanity.

When their "peers" have absorbed the idea that because of their last name, their gender, the brownness of their fathers' skin, their mothers' long dark hair, and the perceptions about their social class, among several other points of "contention," they are presumed less than, other, not the "You/Me" the song refers to.

And while my determination is fierce, I am saddened by the reality of having to prepare them for battle against these preconceived notions that will be used to justify the exclusion of my guerreras from certain spaces, block their access to resources in areas like health and education, and call on them to show up with constant "proof" of belonging.

In preservation of my sanity, I know I'm not alone in this, and we will keep tapping in to the magic

of the moon and stars,

the strength and grace of our dance,

the legacy of our ancestors,

and the power of speaking our truth

as relatives who belong to this land

Sublimation

We hold

these truths

to be

self-evident

this rumination

reclaimed requiem of emancipation

complex dance of liberation,

legacy in full activation

toward a symphony of incantation,

reflexatory indignation

quite possibly beyond restoration,

a sacrifice of reparations

overdo reconciliations

retroactively disrupting stations

forecasted recalibrations

streaming furies of wise damnation

nullifying fortressed limitations

along with mythologies of our creation

citizens in deportation

recycling repatriation

socialized intimidation

complicity of participation

imaginaries of a nation

ancestors in sublimation

frequencies disrupting stations

undivided agitation

rooted

your spirit is tall

so let it expand

your silence

speaks volumes

so let it demand

a justice long lasting

without a grandstand

your heart loves intensely

so let it command

a remembrance that's rooted

in indigenous land

Derechos

And it's completely our r i t e
in our calling to w r i t e
in order to r i g h t . . .

They force us to fight
overlooking our flight

And it ain't about running
we're rooted and cunning

Been at it so long
because we belong

We push on their box
finding healing with rocks.

And they'll presume
that we've got it all wrong.

Insist and persist
that they know our damn song.

Not knowing

That our rites
aren't just passage;
They're L I F E.

La Facultad Jaguar

A jaguar visited
her in her dreams
Approaching gently
Power. nuzzled free.

A warm caress.
Her body shaken
trembling fear
Soul. reawakened.

The only harm
Lived in her bind
Threatening abscess
Whole being. divine.

Cunning strategic
Tactful refined
All the tools to free
Her. mind.

Recovering self
No invitation
Answering the call

Time. incantation.
Confront this realm
with hair disheveled
Fierce feline mane
Freedom now. reveled.

Absorbing the legacy
Gripping the breadth
Luminous sanity
Fierceness full. depth.

Speaking her truth
Words stir emancipation
Courage and heart
Song reflecting. Liberation.

sahumadora

what of a world
placed in their hands
would we insist
on trampling lands

interning our children
through trauma malignance
disregarded humanity
and normalized indignance

or visions more suited
to what they desire
to be loved and well-rooted
taking care of the fire . . .
                -- sahumadora

Healing Wild Woman

I read some poems about a woman and her wicked ways
    Once.
        Once were warriors. Guerrilleras.
    Cholas. Pachucas. Hechiceras.
    Cabronas, Hociconas, Andariegas.

Words. matter.
    energy trumps
    long buried stumps
    all that remains of the evidence
Swallowed up by mother earth.
    To hide?
    Hardly.

Protecting
    like a time capsule
    until we are ready
        to recover
        our antepasados,
Digging up our roots,
    as we rediscover those messages
        carried
        in our genetic makeup: DNA
        Dando Nuestro Amor

Cellular memory atrophied by time and socialization.

Patriarchy, racism, genocide, colonization.
Strong words.
Hard lines.
No room
for the grey.
Funny how that works.
Words.
Names.
Power.
Embrace your wild woman ways.
Reclaiming what is
rightfully yours

For in the end,

the one with the power is

you.

Hives

Addiction to infliction
    self harm imposed
        through friction
           poking
                at the hornets nest
              Miss-taken boundaries
        for openness
      Repainted narratives
of horns in jest

Revelations of
    aggressiveness
        Passively pursuing
           Rest
        Apologetic rhetorics
    Bypassed
self
--centeredness
    Willfully
        Full reticence
    Declining
All the negligence
    pretenses of fool patience at best
In tending to the tangled nests
                    Releasing
toxic blockages
enmeshed with codependent venomness

Al Hocico Libre

AN HOMENAJE TO WHISPERS SET FREE

Maligned as big and bad. I held my tongue in the moment, swallowed my words, choked on my tears, feeling the waves of years of accumulated grief. In that moment, I held the stories of so many women vilified across space and time for daring to speak their truths while equally and violently scorned for their silence. Women, present and past, who have whispered across tables to weave together collective stories of survival and truth. Women, perfect and flawed, who have been dismissed as chismosas and mitoteras. Menacing women burdened with the unratified intergenerational indentured servitude bestowed upon them as the perpetual containers of deflected accountability. An inconvenient convenience that advances a lopsided permissive dysfunction that leaves us in a perpetual state of checkmate -and the irony of that phrasing is not lost on me. *Siempre para entender y atender.*

When one can wear rage as a right, the significance of a whisper is lost. Disassociated dissonance. Dismissed, decontextualized, distorted, devalued. Demonized. Murdered. We're taught forgiveness and virtue, and it comes at a price.

That night I was accused of whispering. Faith and religion did not go hand in hand. A holy trinity, made only of them - *el padre, el hijo, y el espíritu santo.* Three wise men bearing gifts, all against a backdrop of nurturing mothers, relying on pues no se - some story about a vato named José? Generously shouldering the grace and wisdom to serve and protect so that Maria could birth Chuyito by way of immaculate conception. Givers of life. Christmas. The irony of a day marked by the mythology of a big bearded generous male bearing gifts taking credit for the work of so many others -mothers. Appropriating Santas. Maybe we participate in our own erasure sidelining ourselves because we know that the real magic is in the power of the everyday. Our bones remember the corn mothers, domesticated for the coming of Christ as sacrifice -and the irony of the symbolism is not lost on me. *Siempre para entender y atender.*

That night I was accused of whispering, and I thought of my parents. Their pride and disappointment. How in some way this was my punishment for having survived. Wondering if the pressures of proving their parenting to get it all right was exhausted through all of that teen parent might. So that by the time of my brothers, there grew space for them free. Was it simply a matter of birth order beyond three? The contradictions so severely gendered, it can't be about me. Except that I know women like me elicit a backlash when we speak so freely. Y aquí estamos: *Siempre para entender y atender.*

That night I was accused of whispering and I thought of my daughters because I have no sons, and I'm grateful for their knowledge and respect for the humanity of the they, them, non-binary, non-gendered theirs. I wondered if this display would seep into their bones, poisoning their understanding of masculinity. Or if it would infect their ideas of how women should be treated with nobody interjecting, in spite of a room full of beings. Familia. *Siempre para entender y atender.*

That night I was accused of whispering and I thought of my husband. Six feet tall, brown, brawny, weathered hands who work more than the lands. His exterior fits the bill of what is easily attached to our stereotypes of a macho, de los tóxicos all masculine and muy chingón. Even though he bears less scars, making him less calloused and more inclined to fall into being the nurturing one. Sometimes feels to me like too much softness for three daughters, but maybe that's simply because I'm still learning a less rigid way of parenting: hijas de la chingada, while stumbling through keeping them free from sagas of dramas passed on to and through me. *Siempre para entender y atender.*

That night I was accused of whispering and I thought of my grandparents lost to decades past. Remembered how I prayed to my grandmothers trusting their wholeness beyond their own brokenness, having not had them for nearly enough time. And that one time my abuelito visited me in a dream, spoke no words, offered his hands, twinkling eyes reminding me of the times I summoned strength from a nurturing humorous man. Felt like medicine. And while I'd rather forget my mother's father, I am reminded of the many times he was described as a "good man" and I wonder: how many of us keep those secrets dutifully. *Siempre para entender y atender.*

That night my brother . . . accused me of whispering. A braid of past, present, and future ripped through me. I sat there, tears streaming down my face. His morphed into one of nightmares past. And I wept while choosing silence. In part perhaps silence chose me -as someone who speaks de puro corazón, it's not an easy feat to find words amidst the shattering of a mangled heart. They say trauma lives in the body, passed down, and I hail from a lineage of enlarged corazones. Clearly, not because I have no words, but because I was taught respeto. Of having to be that ejemplo at my own expense. *Siempre para entender y atender.*

That night, I was accused of whispering, and if the rush of blood humming in my ears could speak...tsstss...tsstss... tsstsstsstsstss...it might have formed prayers. No songs of heartbreak could match the rhythm of what sounded like the rezos during a novena for loved ones departed.

Santa Maria Madre de Dios. Pray for the men who fancy themselves keepers of the sacred at our expense. Ruega por nosotros pecadores. Pray for the men who have lost touch with the feminine, fancying their oppressive complicity as essential to their being gentlemen. Prayers for those who learned they only had to love us siendo decente in our roles as mothers while clinging to a lopsided masculinity that remains fragile at best. Ahora y en la hora de nuestra muerte. Amen.

Aye men. Ah, men.

That night I was accused of whispering, and this morning, the women who have carried me in my veins, whispered back. In whispered silence de la tinta sagrada, like others before me, past my mourning. I holler truths righting through writing, re-membering to write whole how we've survived traditions of silence that were never ours to hold. All while being dragged and judged for daring to thrive, and I am reminded that in spite of all threats we remain alive.

Our only conspiracy: haciendo que hacer, sembrando semillas, a living archive, hablando con mi hermana, medicina hecha a mano, de espíritu, sagradas, perpetual midwives.

Our work moving forward:
jubilación
  telling our stories,
re-membering to thrive.

That night I was accused of whispering, I remembered myself. Centered where I came from and who I've become. How once upon a time I was taught to look for others to be full and complete. How much of that was no longer a part of me. Of all the healing salves that helped us heal ourselves. Networks of chosen sisters, nurtured and learned. Re-covering how we tend inwardly. Re-learning to play, hands in the sand, feet in the dirt, messy and grand.

Mujer es. VIDA

DIOSA   LIBRE   SIEMPRE
                          HOLLERING
WHISPERING   BEING   VIVAS

LAS QUEREMOS

coyolxauhqui

trying to stay authentically
true to the me
while folks keep trying to
shake parts outta me
while laying claim to
some wholeness of me
that rightfully belongs
to just me
simultaneously feed
fragmentations of me
that ain't what
I long to be --

          --me

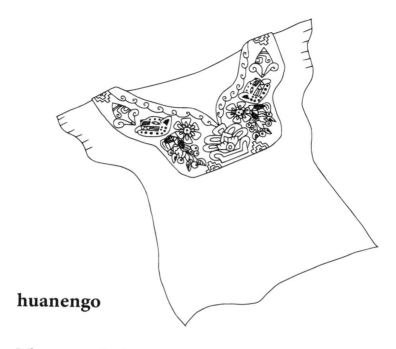

huanengo

When we speak of translations we think of just language

But what of the code-switching cultures and habits

And awareness of presence expressions divine

embracing the woven between heart and mind

those reflexes that are learned to do more than survive

And the capacity to know from those intersticios to thrive

Chiasmus

COMO CHISMES IN TRUTH WHEN
THERE'S TRUTH IN THE CHISMES

It's not the words of the fool,
but the fool with the words

It's not the promise of the action,
but the action in the promise

it's not the hood of the homegirl;
it's the homegirl from the hood

it's not the women in the skirts
but the skirting of the women

it's not the swagger in my step;
it's the step in my swagger

it's not the ego in the purpose,
but the purpose of the ego

it's not the flowers in my language;
it's the language of my flowers

It's not the truths that are spoken,
but what's spoken as the truth

it's not the drum with the beats;
it's the beat of the drum

it's not the danzante with the pasos,
but the pasos de danzante

it's not the dream of the artist;
it's the artist with the dream

it's not the path that we forge,
but the forging of a path

it's not a journey for the power;
it's the power in the journey

And, it's not how we live to survive;
it's how we survive to come alive.

All Ironies Intended
A POEM FOR THOSE WHOSE EXISTENCE IS RESISTANCE

A refined rage reflex
peppered with inappropriate humor
marinated in a truth beyond me

mujeres on the microphone
recycling colonized ideals
internalized fundamentalist trinkets
      repeating formulas of censorship:
      dic'que "calladita te ves mas bonita"
      amplifying senseless noise
      claiming to give voice
      blurring out the true expense
      our non-marketable traits
      discarded as nonsense

tucked into appropriated rebozos
obligating silence toward protection
of our brown brothers
      Loyalist essentialist
      for the nonviolent cause
      Romanticized movement
      Illuminating whitewashed liberation
      Examining socializations too
      identify complicitness
      easy institutions blamed

Never once stopping to see
that buildings without people
are empty boxes filled with things

según misunderstandings of my cultura
victimize machista brothers
for they know not what they do
sisters, keepers
of the fire
sahumadoras
offering blessings
shielding, sweeping, clearing, absorbing

that the education of our people
we must shoulder
because we are
the *givers of life*
with sacred wombs
for the offering
nurturing breasts
  for the taking
  of a borderline people
  thriving in the grey
  boundaries demarcated
  for safe-keeping
  enter oppressors
  with facets of me
  walls manipulated
  into meaningless superfluousness

See, we've been here before
with exception
        mujeres before us
        Resisting the burial
        having screamed
        baring testament
        bleeding stories
        in the permanence of ink

retrofitting memories of
this master's house never
intended to be home
uninvited reverse in-filtration
intentionally provoking
rhetoric and jargon choking
the life out of the living
teaching masters of oppression
facades of success at our expense

so mija remember this:
        hocicona eres más chingona
        speak truth to power and resist
        revolution is you

                        –in the fullness of your bliss.

Rosie's Revenge

CON RESPETO DON "CORKY" GONZALES, QEPD

Mis respetos Don Corky
 –Gonzales, to boot
I've got poems in my repertoire
and boxing gloves too.

And while we've
inter-generationally
centered, glorified, and canonized
el mijo *Joaquin*
lost in a world of confusion,
I constantly
find myself
battling
a landscape
of erasure and collusion.

Forced into margins,
footnotes and ibids…
called so many names
'cause we've never been silent

See . . .
There's a clarity in that gap,
it's a hole

in the fabric
where we keep
snagging at the facade
like a tenacious rabid maverick.

Chronically gaslit.
Braided and suited.

Released the mantilla
of the suffering woman.
Polished long-lost armas
forcibly removed,
dug hands in the dirt
excavated
what was buried.

Reclaimed my copilli
while barefoot
like the Rarámuri.

Perfected –my aim
be-cause we've never
been tame.

Convinced us our ego
hungered for fame,
preyed on and violated,
toward humbly silent.

Weaponized prayers.
Entangled affairs.
Compartmentalized saints and sinners,
displayed for the stares.

Labeled vendidas
while you pay for the chairs.
Tokens and bounty
for prophets and winners.
Where all the world's a stage
and everyone loses.

More than profits,
It's life.
No bruises,
just muses
and sanctified wombs.
Over-regulated ovaries.
Disemboweled, entombed.
Declared
—sacred.
 victims.
 insane.
Containers and targets
of unnecessary hate.

Despite all that spite,
we find ways
to bloom.

We're warriors
Re-member[ed].
> encoded heirlooms

somos gente,
complex, perfect, and flawed
dismembered, embodied,
at times broken and clawed

abrasively ravenous
simultaneously
selfishly selflessly
unequivocally broad

Concomitantly
Imperfectly
Indisputably

We.

Listen,
we'll tell you...

ibid

…..ibid:
We're warriors.
−scratch: ~~warriors~~
human: somos gente,
complex, perfect, and flawed

Re-member[ed].
−scratch: ~~Re-member[ed].~~
dismembered, embodied,
at times broken and clawed

Encoded heirlooms
−scratch: ~~Encoded heirlooms~~
abrasive and ravenous
simultaneously selfish and selfless
the range is so broad

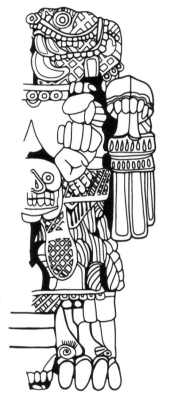

dig. uncover.
dig. recover.
dig. revisit.
dig. repeat.

repeat.   repeat.   repeat.   repeat.
dig. uncover. dig. recover. dig. revisit.
dig.
repeat.

But did you read it?
PRESUMED INCOMPREHENSIBLE

The most annoying question posed in all of its variants after a woman [read non-white] speaks up about contradictions in perspectives:

But did you read it?

Triggers in me . . .

a response I've sat with in full familiarity; makes me wonder if they've sat and held themselves in critical introspection long enough to see the hint of assumptions it carries about narratives so robustly problematically enabled by the brutality of our actual history and currently gaslit collective reality

the smell of stale buildings, bleached out tables, dusty plaques, mildewed certificates

in perpetuity, cyclically,
coding on complicity,
targeting aggressively

the taste of swallowed tears as we nurture children back to brilliance beat out of them by systems insistent on branding their deficits

because we
must hail from . .

an illiterate expendable, somehow intellectually incapable,
comprehension unobtainable, exceptionally unrelatable,
never actually debatable, perpetually dismissible, chronically
erasable, absolutely reprehensible

                                        . . . them or that

stay grounded and rooted

in collective we . . .

cognitively, somatically, thoroughly, resiliently, exhaustedly
responsively, responsibly, abundant in ferocity, through lack of
reciprocity, speaking

                                        --with audacity.

Chingona Fierce

I am chingona fierce

I wonder when they'll realize

I am not here to hold their space

declining submissive container of twisted knots

and rusted nails of discarded discord of discontent

I hear the song of a thousand grandmothers before me

whisper as the ocean roars

I see the stillness of the moon reflecting

wisdom piercing steady light

guiding clarity amongst a star struck night

I want to gather in collective truth

manifesting justice

even when

it's just us

I am chingona fierce

I pretend nothing as I pack

un-be-longing into your walls

I feel the fractures of broken exteriors

Shards of glass fragilities

reminding me of why I am feared

I touch the wounds with the healing medicine

of the brujas, curanderas, sobadoras

before me resurrecting

authenticity to life

I worry exhaustion will swallow me whole,

devour all bravado

lull me into a commodified illusion of contentment

forgetting to live

neglecting to thrive

I cry sacred tears of wild woman rising

on borrowed time

echoing menacing existence

gathering dahlias

blooming in the fullness of our legacy

beyond resilience

I am Chingona Fierce.

Ignited. Unbound. Free.

ocelotl tekpatl

Code-switching reticence
Declining forced beneficence
Defending vested residence

Perpetually privileged petulance
Such ignorance distresses us
Exhausting empty penitence

Fallacious fabled eminence
Sanctions spurious evidence
Fatiguing us toward pettishness

Vested battle pensiveness
To counteract such negligence
Declaring factual innocence

Promulgating rightfulness
To challenge twisted righteousness
Beyond these rhymes there's eloquence

                                        -- in war

war cry

And they made us fight for this
without knowing we're warriors for this
from a literate people for this
as I take in the beauty of this
and they say we aren't made for this
and they can't see the fierceness in us
and it does not matter
what we think of us
because these compulsory spaces of this
exclude all the fullness of us
and they'll deny the fearing of us
of being a literate us
while they keep us fighting with us
instead of advancing as us
and my tears
have flowed deep for all this
and I know
we can
do better . . .
because . . .
THIS.

Do you see?

Beautiful Soul Speak

A town with a snag
Never about a flag
Expecting participation
In our dignity's expatriation

Politics and hate leaving a sour taste
Attempting to seal our fate
Silence the masses
Breed fear in our classes

From Cinco de Mayo
El pueblo sagrado
Her arms outstretched
She speaks to our gente

A poet projects
An activist shines
La danzante enshrines
With a full heart entwines

Swirled in sage and copal,
Esa esencia de saguaro nopal:
Transcending
Borrowed time
Our people
Caretakers
Working the land

For a peaceful world
Simple and just
Generations before
Sacrificing in trust

Touching our souls
Ripple effects
Confronting the web
Grace and eloquence

The right of the people.
Tears beckoning
Pride. Honor. Dignity
Humanidad reckoning

For our children.
Peace.

Tlatlatziniliztli *OSÉA, THUNDER*

Post danza midnight reflections
on some patterned dysfunctions
  --maybe I've been reading too much
    Lorde, Anzaldúa, and Castillo;
  or maybe I've been
  serendipitously connecting
    with too many stories
    that weave together
    a constellation
    of truths;
  or maybe, I'm just
    tired . . .
    because
    my thoughts
    rumble like prayer,
  expanding like thunder

Orenda *POWER BEYOND PURPOSE*

So many shiftings
Long overdue siftings
Beyond any mysteries
In touch with rich histories
Intentionally drifting
Decidedly gifting

- Purpose

And Still, We Braid

digging for erasers
unbeknownst
how past erasures
have us digging
for raw stories
hearts and minds
our fullness craving

pumping gas
and grocery shopping
stand in line
at checkstand 5
notice history
got us hyphy
cuz some bodies
ain't treated rightly

and they tell us
we've got lyrics
maybe dabble
in some Limericks
they won't pay us
for our time
bleed our hearts
make our existence
codified transgressive crime

weaponizing roses
while they're
elevating Moses
and they sure
can't keep their noses
out of compromising poses

don't want us thriving
past resistance
nearly gentrifying co-existence
subjective agents of persistence
stripping knowledge
welcome sorrow
disconnect us
from our rhymes

-- and still . . .
      we braid.

Gente Decente

If you listen closely, you can hear it
almost of a hum, the swoosh of the drum

bridging across space and time
reverberating stories
of this land, survival, resilience,

Joy through hostility
A constellation of so many beautiful we's
Stories of sacrifice, imposed resilience
Calloused hands, stiffened backs

Our grandmothers
Seven generations forward
And seven generations back
Of gente remembered
Connected to the land
Babies who howl at the moon
and handmade tortillas
better than any spoon.

You see, my grandmothers Ruth and Mercedes carried poetry
in their names, birthed poetry past all of their pains.
From El Limón, Michoacán and Las Cruces, Nuevo México,
stories encoded in these very veins.

Del rancho y del campo, they held my hands
through these very streets,
mighta swerved in some of these lanes,
celebrated with ranchera beats.

De gente decente
a few with names etched into stone

past the ones we already know
out in Santa Paula, for the riches of citrus they never owned.
and the photographs of marching with those red little flags
made their way north where the sun never lags

Mushroom plant stories to circuit board glories.
Del Monte canneries, nevermind their salaries.

And the drum, the drum,
it still calls on me
syncs up with the heartbeat
anchors my sanity
tugs on my rusty feet
reminding me
to connect with planted seeds
Sometimes mistaken for hostile weeds.

Calls on me to
            RE-MEMBER;
            REMEMBER MIJA, REMIND THEM

Chinga Tu Afterthought

We are not an after-thought
We are an exclamation
My standing here
-- an affirmation
My ancestors resistance
turned reclamation

Surviving and thriving in spite of Indignation
My rhymes, a scathing song of Liberation
Refusing artificial boundaries of Trepidation

Chola scholars defying all shortsighted expectation
Scientific processes shamefully advancing our damnation
Enter Guerrilla Poets aligning overdue reconciliation

We've risen beyond waves across space and time
of these chronically misconstrued timelines

Existing phenomenally
Giving Life
como la luna
controlling the tides

Where we come from
is so much more than a well-manicured glass house
politicized beyond the lies

We are   a people
                                of cultura y corazón
Herederas de círculos
                                where the hummingbird flies
Reminding us that
                                in spite of all pretense
we continue to rise.

Centering ourselves
while battling critiques of self-centeredness
when that centering is essential
to acknowledging our sacredness.

Carrying where we come from
and who we've always been.
Hearts with Eastside roots
marching while grieving all of our missing and murdered
            warriors --women

Amplifying stories
Tucked under the cadence of un/be-longing
Here with fists up as we declare
            a long-standing legacy collectively affirming
            the recycled poetry of this:
                    that who you carry is who carries you
                    seven generations forward
                    and seven generations back;
                    bypassing artificial wisdom
                                As keepers of truth.

Censura

sequestered receipts

concealed

without monuments

uncommissioned

precarious pendulums

disappearing ink

reflectivity perpetually

redundantly appallingly

incessantly on repeat

- hoodwinked

Center Justified

I would never

not I

it's the system

they cry

center

some privilege

weaponize

why

appropriation

of knowledge

intellectual

standby

Just People, Though

Institutions without people
... empty boxes filled with things
Buildings bearing witness
To the messes conjured behind scenes
Surveillance through plantation se[e]ms
distressingly oppressively
Adopted unceremoniously
calendared codependent rituals
[In]action conditioned on perpetuals
Strike
A chord
Calculated hold
slightly out of tune
dysfunctional historical
perhaps uncategorical

Those hands are tied
Just compromise
Consent always somehow implied
A tethering untendering
Exacting unnecessarily
taxing while distractingly
Invariably on bartered time

The Institution
... slow to change

The people though...
Just people, though

Maintain the chains
Bulldoze, arraign
Rebrand, rebuild,
While practices
remain the same

Both signed and authored by ...

The people, though...
Just, people though

The Institution
... slow to change

Unceremonious Mitote

To the women in perpetual preemptive strike mode,

    I am not here for you.

My journey is one of liberation

    --with a mural of folks

    I am compelled to remain accountable to

    and whose legacies I live for.

To the women who lash out first to beat us to the punch,

    I refuse to hold your accountability

    while you avoid the mirror of actual threat.

My journey is one of humanity and compassion

    -- with a world full of folks

    who are rooted in love.

To the women who are constantly strategizing forward

while claiming to have to watch their backs,

    I decline your invitation to engage in your spiral.

My journey is one of gathering hearts

    --with a community of corazón

    that collectively uplifts.

To the women who confuse empathy and compassion

for a soft vulnerability in need of tempering,

    I remind you that I was forged in a fire

    tempered by stories beyond your conception.

My journey has molded me into more than just resilience

    --with life giving stories of both tenderness and pain.

To the women with the pitchforks in their hands

masked as allyship and liberation,

    I am compelled to remind you

    that I have survived witch hunts

    throughout so many lives.

My journey is one of a different fight

    -- releasing my traumas

    to gather the light.

encaje

some open doors

not meant for us

our entry

reaches back

tugging on ancestors

reclaiming medicine

pulling through

threads of in/justice

- encaje

cae mal, caiman

Mass importation with mass deportation.

Hostile incarceration alongside cultural appropriation.

Indignation and ongoing degradation.

Crocodile tears of inclusive cooptation.

Celebrations trademarked by corporations.

Displacement by way of expectations.

Unreciprocated accommodations.

Gaslighting all need for reconciliation.

Burying traces of repatriation.

Past due delinquent reparations.

Some sentiments are worth re-stating:

            Our land was never for sale,

       and our muertos are not for the taking.

They Mean

When someone says go back to where you came from and I look at 'em confused because it took a constellation of journeys for me to disrupt this space. I scratch my head and ponder whether they meant...

The halls of Yerba Buena High School, the barbed wire fences of J.W. Fair long rebranded as Bridges Academy. Tully, Story, McCreery, McLaughlin, Capitol, or the pulgas on Sunday?

The semiconductors that preceded Silicon Valley, the canneries of Del Monte, the fields from Morgan Hill to Gilroy, or the citrus groves that built the KKK peppered roadways surrounding Santa Paula, California;

Perhaps they meant the trains and roadways my great grand-mother trekked West ahead of her time leaving a trail behind, the bridges and railroads her son built with his hands because while nobody ever taught him to read, his sister was busy holding buckets at school, enduring lashings for her spirited protest of refusing to give up her native [Spanish colonizer] tongue;

Maybe, they meant the line where they sprayed my grandfathers with pesticides before they made their way to patch the labor of the lands;

Perhaps that specific border checkpoint lane where my abuelita stealthily smuggled herself in the trunk of a car to establish a legacy of family haphazardly unified –if you ask me, that's essential contraband.

Maybe I could journey further south if I could decide where the bended knurled fork points simultaneously across the border and to where the border crossed us, adding to that complexity, it's not that big of a mystery.

Maybe, it's Smelter Town of El Paso and the cemeteries not too far from the Rio Grande, or zip past El Chuco, plains and deserts, down dusty highways, aiming for that Oro Grande, or landing in Las Cruces, Nuevo Mexico to pay homage to my grandmother's lands.

Maybe it's not what they meant
It's what they mean

Lost track of the dispossessed native lands
back when
they were boarding up babies
to kill the Indian and save the man

Maybe trek down south from there
Not quite sure exactly where

My Great Grandma said
they'd traveled
back and forth
from Chihuahua
Came across
a document
once read something like
'the man was red'
Not sure how
to follow that mystery thread
when that part of the story
was buried somewhere
Dead?

Maybe it's not what they meant
It's what they mean

Maybe they mean the other path
The fork or branch
more familiar
with the aftermath

That one that traces roads down south.

In places finally traced by maps. Like somewhere in
Jalisco that welcomes me as a guest, gives me nicknames like
trenzuda, gabacha, and pocha as I ponder my own alienness.
Even so, not sure they see Guadalajara the way I do with its
cultured landscapes, complex traits, museums, danza too.

Maybe it's not
what they meant
It's what
they mean

Maybe they mean that dip in the road that always announced
when my dad made it home to El Limón in Michoacán. It's
a different kind of hot there, you can feel it in the land. Or
the river that flowed abundantly once joined so many stories,
kinda feels like a heartland.

Maybe it's not
what they meant
It's what
they mean

Perhaps they mean all the way back across oceans and time . . .

It's the narratives
they mean, I guess

But I know.

I know
they mean

Oh.
They mean.

It's not about where
        - they mean
Or what
        - they mean

Don't care
about papers
like the ones weaponized
green cards, passports, Real IDs
burdens of proof all fall on me

Or those reclaimed
like the ones
my dad's tía
traveled down to trace
a branch in his lineage
to the unclaimed
Europeans

Not those

Because
        - they mean:

Not you.

How do I explain
when they don't care
to listen
when they say
go back to where you came from

                    I'm already here

              When I carry place

                    in my veins

                        as part

                      of the land

                    I'm already here

When we already know:

        –They mean.

Strategic All(Lies)

I write poems
about allies
uncensored words
in full sensory awareness
tucked away
like
empty shells
of diplomacy

there is
no safe
keeping
save for the secrets
discarded
children's bodies
insulating walls
forcibly removed
splintered beams
bore witness
way back
slave labor
no obstruction
to construction
on stolen lands

way back
still trees
fully manifested
lynchings

called it
justice

and our grief

doesn't know
where
to begin
tucked away
changes our DNA

watch yourself
no missteps
tone-policed
tempered tempers
show: respect
suspicious subjects
call me when
… you're home
hands on the steering wheel
do you know
who
… I am

because
they showed up
asking
what more
do you want
teach us
carry this

as they white out
our names

butcher our mothers'
grandmothers
great shame

trauma vultures
circling
carving names
commemorating greatness
on plaques

appropriating accolades
circling
internal memos
to covertly defame

and our rage

doesn't know
where
to begin

so, I write poems
about allies
uncensor
my words
in full
sensory awareness
tuck them away
like
empty shells
of diplomacy

and I know

I am not safe

Pearly Gates

When they beam with pride for having uplifted Dolores Huerta but can't name farmworkers in their community and reluctantly tolerate activists, barely, maybe, pretend, pretentious, pretense, nudging her out, *this work's not for you,*

they've never seen us in the streets, devalue the voice of community, *porque no somos iguales,* forget who was there too, pretend they've never furrowed their brow as they softly talk over you, so they can . . . *give voice,*

while adoring the work of Frida Kahlo, with hands to chest and concerned puppy dog eyes, there's no room for the Chicana artist across the table and zooming to your left, something about how the people need something they can relate to, maybe less abrasive, less angry, (less you?),

while genuinely concerned with barriers and access, whitewashing the issues,

it's easier to swallow that way.

la clave

When you're not "made to believe" anything . . .
because you have direct line access to actual
people the atrocities are happening to,
because you are firm in the systemic analysis of the facts,
because you are rooted in history
while aware of the politic of that narrative,
because you understand the nuanced distinction
between politic and politics,
because you're committed to a collective liberation
and the accountability of us,
because you constantly interrogate your own choices
and habits of complicity in this dysfunction,
because they will come for you
under the guise of seeking to understand
while falling tone deaf to the symphony you embody,
because beliefs are not fixed nor imposed
but constructed, chosen, and politicized
because you do not owe an explanation
to those who insist on the imposition of their privilege

because every day is a choice to re-member
who we be   beyond a belief.
                                    in your agency,
                    explicitly, imperfectly, collectively.

En Protesta

Crocodile thick skin
for crocodile tears
of supposed
"no se puede"

of digital destitution
scholars screaming
decades deep
"sí se tiene"

y ahora si,
la gente
unequivocally confirming
"sí se quiere"

legislators on
scrollwork floors
affirming
disregarded receipts
pretentiously discarded
"si se requiere"

all against
a tezcatlipoca haze
urgently reclaiming

we been on that
legacy of
"sí se puede"

La Huerta.
de vuelta.
en plena
protesta.
Para la gente.
Que quién
contesta.

Justicia
en lucha.
Siempre
se cuenta.
Cobrando
abogando.

Guerreras
          -- trucha.

Against Your Window

Against your window,
You can't stand the rain

Trickles down
to nowhere
Never washed
that stain

Tinged hands
exchange lives

Hypersexualized

Hyper Intellectualized
Perpetually
decontextualized
Historically
Over-Dramatized
Dismissively
Stigmatized

U.s.

But you,
Against your window,

You can't stand the rain

Took the land, the water,
displaced homes,
sold a dream too
distracted from the servitude
structured and internalized
as gratitude

Orchestrated
artificial drought
bludgeoned burdened
Stimulated doubt
Situated landscapes
Monopolized
emotion
Appropriated
trail of tears
Harnessed
Weaponized
and
Racketeered

Because
Against

Your window

You
won't stand.

The Rain.

context con leche

the rogue
coffee bean
finds its way

into a tazita de barro
swirling in a cup of milk

- never mind

how much
processing
it takes
to get it
that
artificially white

the milk
is not itself either

saladita

Celebrating representations
In contradicting ostentations
reprimanding indignation
Provisional professionalizations
Authenticity in full damnation
Allyship toward criminalization
In service toward false sense of nation
Recycling notions of colonization

This poem is grounded
In all the salty dedications . . .

Static

colonizer cameos
disrupting how I dream
stuck
  in a classroom
  ironically
a space
that's brought
some joy to me

kept saying things
so openly
quite Truthfully
perpetually
repeatedly
exhaustedly

No, no, said she
  self-appointed
  pale authority
made sure
to stand on
over me

head of class

instructively
condescending
diminishingly
dismissively
      'cuz she
      was the authority

of us and we
      and our history
and our currency
and our currently
collectively
      gaslit
      harsh reality

collecting paychecks
      so eagerly
      upon "mere stats"
a numbers game
      It's just our backs
and stacks
      of opportunity
rhetoric
likes
community

Tortilla Consciousness

strip away
the parts of me
of which your statistical norms
don't seem to agree

"peel my love
like an onion"
leaving a stench of injustice
misaligned with the values that are we

hack away the leaves
and destroy the seeds
of consciousness
leave no trace of unacceptable unruliness

shape, assess, and mold
enforcing the status quo
take comfort in diminishing
dancing to a culture of zero tolerance

mold into toxicity
making it so that I can't breathe
poison minds with doubt
stifling sacred purpose throughout

silence this rage
that I've honored within my spirit
silence this voice
that I've fine tuned over the years
to articulate myself against the injustice
imposed by those who would beat
my soul into submission
command me
to stand in line
with the others and lower
my eyes
close
my eyes
to what is going on
around me

strip me of my dignity?
NO.
Because I rise.

I rise
like a warm flour tortilla
bubbling on the comal
ready to create that comfort
ready to be more than just consumed
turning my gifts into energy
an energy that fuels
an energy that invigorates

While Mami is making mambo,
this mami is making revolution.

Resisting your perfect form
refusing to become
a tool of your oppression
Declining to recreate the injustice
that I seek to rise against
as I seek to enlist warriors
in a struggle
as we build consciousness together
creating a critical mass of critical minds

We do not bow our heads
remaining silent
passive to your efforts

We speak, we rise, we shout, we stand
Demand and Command
DIGNITY
INTEGRITY
with swagger.
y que

Monumental

poems are debatable, you know.

like flags . . .
and people . . .

they say you repeat what you need to learn
--seems more like an imposition to me

kinda like all them mythologies...
history, heroes, men on horses...

the allies who took the time to show up
and then forgot to listen

even when el llanto took to the streets, screaming.

La Llorona centuries deep.

                    Let's build her a monument

                              -make it white.

Raised to Rise

"I didn't raise you like that"
- Except you did.
Growing up with your example,
Knowing
I didn't want to be you.
Determined
Not to be you.
Struggling to survive
Sometimes
In spite of you.
Refusing
To keep my mouth shut
Swallowing and wallowing
In pride
Shackled in a box,
Dimmed by the shadows,
Haunted by acceptance.
Freedom out of grasp.
Until I learned the battle
Was with myself.
La hija buena
Siendo la hija de la chingada
La niña obediente
Contra la cabrona rezongona.
But wait,

Oh the weight,
That realization
Keeping me in chains.
Lighter
In transformation.
Clarity in the journey.
Simmering,
Until boiled over in rage,
Seething with fury,
Passed on through generations.
Weeping. Surrendering. Empowering.
All the same.
Struggling to find peace
With your ways,
As I learn to embrace
The depth of your grief
With compassion
Healing the scars.
You were sacrificed
Forced to survive.
While your child screams

Demanding:

WE THRIVE

Contentious

"You've got a chip on your shoulder."
But it's not a chip
And it hardly resides
on these shoulders of mine

Allow me to elaborate
About the 42+ mile gaping crevice
Threatening to unravel
"this bridge called my back"
 scarred territory
covered by the bandage
that is my baggage
chartered by the legacy of rage
infracted by transgressions of aggression
impacted by the violation of my nation
compacted by the collective susto of my gente
retracted by the filtered remedios of my youth

a part of me grew
wary of the time
tried to break
my spirit
while division and derision
threatened
my peace

innocence marred
haunted substratum
a perpetual why
yet soul patched the wounds
spotted like the jaguar
that is me
clinging to the earth
alive and free

So excuse me
while I correct
the misconception
align
my spine
with the beauty
of my twine

finding solace
in the swearing
lately
I find
myself
wearing

my battle scars
with pride.

Rarámuri

I don't run anymore
puzzled, frazzled,
scarred, and scared
stillness still
out of reach
gripping white knuckled
knapsack
a tattered hand-me-down
untraceable
always detectable
constantly cut
at the seams
hollowed out
helped themselves
replaced it with
a promissory note
read "privilege"

I don't run anymore
Re-tired
those running shoes
bare foot
danzante
uncalloused
where it counts

Drum Speak

Thinking 'bout my day
         as I lace up through the fray
drums in the background,
         speaking in the foreground
tenacious mourning
conjuring. returning
sifting, sorting,
the displaced funk.
Refusing the absorbing.
--it's all bunk.
Life. too short. Refusing drama.
         Esta ruca es una dama
spare a few
from my words
the temptation feels absurd
free these old friends. Door's ajar
cut and sting and leave a scar.
Tlazoltéotl as my guide
Four Agreements turned divine
insults swirling through my mind.
my resolve so damn refined.
Journey healing seals my fate
Freeing me from senseless hate
The revolution takes a stance, demanding that I . . .
         Don't walk. Dance.

Beyond Sepia Tones

¿Te acuerdas de las veces que te dije
que las calladitas son las mas cabroncitas?
        we meant it as a compliment,
        an affirmation of the force you've always been
        --because you come from us, from way back when.

blessed you with an abundance of family
        that sometimes feels like a burden
        because their energy is duality and might
        imposing both heavy and light

We know they built that ferocity into you
        sometimes force fed it to you
        'til the weight of the fullness grew
        moulding a spirit to shape-shift
        by way of a perpetually powerful brew

And re-membering is both that space that you hold
and the space that holds you.
        So, re-member that wildness you carry in your heart.
        And re-member your light to re-member your joy,

while you balance tears of sorrow beyond happenstance
        Remember that life
        is an on-going dance

Precious

they say knowledge is power
and believe we're content
when our children make do
with potential unspent

obstructing all justice
and training for busy
banning the stories
while testing 'em dizzy

well-versed in resilience
keeping it muddled
relentless resistance
leaving them puzzled

culture is wise
precious and true
reconciliation in books
--hope's reflection of you
                    -quetzalcoatl

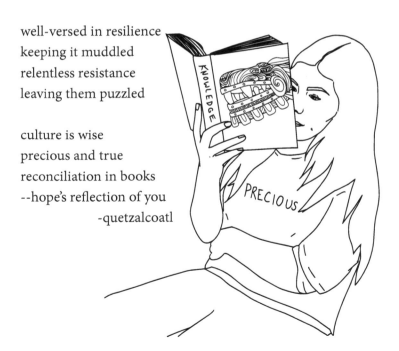

Control-Alt-Delete

great men with their dreams distorted painted over white like
the Payless mural on Story Road non-surgically methodically
snipped non-consensually insipidly dismissively onward
to the next sale reminds me of the simultaneously nimble
strong hands who built this valley both for the silicon and
heart's delight bet they had dreams too pictures fade into
boxed memories like the folks who showed up on bicycles
in protest for what should have never been a constellation of
cancellation with chronically renewed unapproved
subscriptions on auto pay from a stolen account can't be used
for anything else necessitating in perpetuity indenturedly
belabored-ly recovering affirmingly resisting the tendency to
hurriedly conceal all discrepancy

while women have dreamed too

no breaks, no lines, no room

I Dream

I dream of a world   where my daughters can run free
Safe in notoriety,   or perhaps   chosen anonymity

A world where   "call me when you get home" can be
more about   that good, good tea
than about   fearing   for our safety,

A world where   all bodies   are somebody valued

I'll say it again:
A world   where all bodies
are somebody   valued

F R E E

in identity, expression,   and questioning,
Beyond threatening,   reckoning,   –perhaps beckoning
Remembering,   welcoming,   strengthening

I dream of safe places being   reality
Inclusivity   unquestioning our
Trans, queer, and gender nonconforming   humanity

A world where flyers with the words M I S S I N G
Are non-existent unless . . .

they're about friendships   and forgiving

Where our kids can learn words   like grooming
as simply meaning
          the practice of keeping
          a neat and tidy appearance (as choice).

A world   where I   don't have to
catch my tears in my throat as mentors share stories
of how   that one time   in a movie theater
is part of shared memoir;

I'm tired,   I'M TIRED, y'all

Remembering back   to how we all stepped in
to the circle confirming #metoo
What I'd give
to not carry
those stories
of what we've been through

A world   where I   don't have to
walk around guarded,
with a look signifying   you might just catch hands,
Keeping all   of my senses intact
when the world is insistent   on violence
through a myriad of cosigned and coded conscripted
Likely preventable nonsensical acts

A world where   my keys   can stay tucked in my bag
and babies don't lose   their mothers   to their dads;
I meant
h e r   l i f e
and I didn't mean   to make   y'all sad

Outraged, anxious, gaslit   --still mad

I'd much prefer:

                                    Believed, trusted, protected,
A L I V E ,   and still rad

Sacred, respected, nurtured and whole
Where folks aren't misgendered
and bodies   aren't patrolled,
extorted, trafficked, controlled,
or even dismissively   --cajoled

Where first kisses are sweet memories
that don't involve assault
Where we are not made to believe   it must all somehow
be your fault
            'cuz   what were you wearing,
            how unchecked was your daring
            Your naivete was   so glaring

I mean,
I dream –

I dream –
A dream so vivid, I can feel it, sense it, believe it and see it:
Where people are valued, empowered, and bold

The ancestors -they say we don't have to struggle to learn;
It's about how we learn to remember

Perhaps the pieces of our shared dreams can be prophecy
And in this work consent is key, so:
Will you dream with me and remember?

A world where all bodies
          are somebody valued, empowered, and bold

Where the legacy of this work is action demanded
Embodied in cause, because,
this work
is poetry in some kind of way

And this invitation turned invocation today,
To Dream   and remember:
A world
          where all bodies are somebody
          valued,
          combining those embers
          Toward a world
          where we can all feel nurtured, grown tender

Where people are valued, empowered, and bold.

109

capaz

How do you parent
a capable body
to be more than
some body
while also instilling
the value of bodies
taken for granted
the power of bodies
to speak?

                    - disability

And where can we push
as enabled bodies
beyond falsification
of able-bodies
when this mythology
privileges bodies
devaluing spirit
perfecting bodies
of chronic neglect?

                    - impairment

And why can't our language
embrace all the bodies?
anomalous deviance
rebellious in-bodied
Imperfectly perfect
Holistic in bodies
Sparing compassion
The body is Somebody
        As is.
        - PERSON

Dear Strong Woman

I've seen poems for the mama
who worries about her body
in size and in years

All kinds of assumptions
absorption of standards
seen only through regrets
reinforcing perfection
through imposed imperfections
reassured she is enough
superhumanly tough

But what of the mama
who fears for her body
no hate for the mirror
no lies that she fears
the reflection straight rooted
in generations of folks
who've fought for belonging
who flawed in their longing
unique combinations unend
in creational blends

Poems that remind me
that I can spit fire
but what about tears?

to cleanse
all the toxins
absorbed through the years
of traumas preceding
sifting through fears
to summon the strength
when the health of a body is unclear

Not the size or the skin
It's the physically aching
Unidentified cause
Perhaps wildly mistaken

To be
Simply human
Surviving and thriving
Without ever tucking
And swallowing down
Emotionally spiritually
Beyond physicality
Full bodied and flawed
In our humanity
Never been small

This one's for the mama
who fears for her body
afraid it's not enough
to last all the years
to lend all the ears
mend babies' fears
when they're all grown
and out on their own
with uncertain timelines
and bodies on lien
without guarantees

Of years or of days
Roar past the fatigue
Not allowed to be tired
Because "Girl, you are fire!"

It's not fire I want
It's time to just breathe

And permission to be

Feel
all my emotions
In waves,
like the ocean

That are
        - perpetually me

copal

And what if the well of her rhymes should run dry?
Will her need to scream truths compel her to try?
And how will she translate what words can't quite say?
Will that pesky impostor syndrome lead her astray?
Or will she stay rooted, ferocious, and firm
Precise in her language, while gracious and stern,
Tenaciously articulating a wholeness confirmed
Beyond metaphors that leave you intentionally perturbed?
In truth, it's a legacy that runs undisturbed
Rumbling in her veins majestically well-preserved.

Mujeres de Posteridad

The poetry of our wicked ways.
    Wonder women.
        Guerrilleras.
    Love. Spirit.
        Community.
    Mujeres de posteridad.

Palabra poderosa
untattered in the trenches.
Split and navigating the nepantla state

We work. We toil.
    For social good.
Planting seeds, watering plants,
stirring up
    the soil.
Not afraid to dirty our hands
    – with the healing spirit of the earth
    esa madre tierra that grounds us.

Women of intellect.
    Mujeres de acción.
Promising, caring,
pero abrasive al igual.
    We scare people

and we don't care.
Except when we care too much
our hearts bleeding, our souls yearning.
For justice. True justice.
Beyond empty rhetoric.

With babies in tow,
We sacrifice. We cry.
Watering the earth with our tears.
Esperanza. Cambio. Poesía.

Tragic bright lights whose hearts are left heavy,
knowing that we are summoned in time.
Still we expand. Ask a physicist.
The huehuetl speaks and the truth is in the capirotada.

For the journey continues, mis compañeras.
With your energía surrounding us.
Branching out in an eternal embrace.
Pushing us forward to follow our hearts.

Taking courage. Corazón.
Deciding and defining.
Depth. Journey. Hope. Faith.
Proof. We are reflections of each other.
Leaders. Adelitas. Fuerza.

Make it count.

Un-Preyed

Pray for the ones that don't understand how the ceremonial ways are inextricably bound with the sacredness of women amidst the sanctity of ceremony, whose internalized relationship with propriety stripped of the erotic runs deep. Pray for the ones who live these ways with the best of intentions while privilege affords them an overlooked elevation of binaried framings of unattainable purity at the expense of our collective humanity. Pray for the ones that confuse the erotic for the pornographic, while failing to understand that the erotic is essentially pure love, joy, and spirituality while living in complete alignment with spirit. Pray for the ones that misinterpret our ability to give life as limited to biology and physiology because it is so much more. Sometimes we give birth to ourselves. Pray for the ones who are chronically uncomfortable with the sacred feminine because it permeates the everyday. Pray for the men who take offense at women harnessing their own medicine by way of the power of heyoka to heal and connect, to laugh, to activate joy and resilience to help us see past the smoking mirrors. Pray for the men who shame the women for making light of the context of chronic trauma we have remained complicit in by policing women's medicine. Pray for the men who have lost touch with the feminine as a part of themselves; a lopsided masculinity is a fragile one at best. Pray for the men who fancy themselves keepers of the sacred at our expense.

parteras partidas

Did you know
poems have birthdays?

It's true
--they do.

Age
in cycles
speaking
a-cross
     space
     and time.
Re-currently
     unpacking
     unmasking
     perpetually
     shifting
     fatigued
     for the
     multi-tasking

meaning
contingent
     on who
     is asking
sometimes
hiding
from
the seeking
in plain
sight

seasoned
technicolor
prisms
reflecting
back light
rebirthing
unearthing
   -- givers of life

Givers of Life

Who takes care of the mothers
while we are busy giving life?

And I remember.

a friend
who hugs
wholeheartedly
embracing
openness
of tender heart
just enough
firmness
to center you back
inward

Apapachando

across distance and time
realizing remembrance
embracing ourselves
encrypted notches
loss and grief
and rage

In piece

feels like
miscarried love
contorted justice
protected
tucked within
soft bodies
cradling so many

Pulling through

Apapachada

mothers midwives
reborn
from ourselves

Just. Us.
Re-membered
Whole.

salve

imagine a world
where everyone owned
the poetry that flows in their veins
every word spoken
would leave us less broken
tending with heart to our pains
we might swallow less truths
be less harsh with our youths
more merciful in our refrains
imagine a world
where everyone owned
the poetry that flows in their veins . . .

NOTES

Code-switches throughout are rarely italicized. In addition to titles and such, italics are used throughout to emphasize a line, phrase, or perhaps a more fluid cadence where applicable.

Opening Quotes

Lorde, Audre. *Sister Outsider: Essays and Speeches.* Crossing Press, 1984, p. 36.

June, Lyla. "Lifting Hearts Off the Ground." *For the Wild Podcast.* Episode 147. 28 Nov. 2019. https://forthewild.world/podcast-transcripts/lyla-june-on-lifting-hearts-off-the-ground-147

lara silva, ire'ne. "Cuicalli viii. house of song." *Cuicalli / House of Song.* Saddle Road Press, 2019, p. 88.

Foreword

Walther, Matthew. "Poetry Died 100 Years Ago This Month." *The New York Times.* 29 Dec. 2022. Op-ed. https://www.nytimes.com/2022/12/29/opinion/eliot-waste-land-poetry.html

Obligation Emancipation: An Hocicona Proclamation

First published in *Label Me Latina/o,* Volume IV, Fall 2014.

Jardín de Flores

"A Huitzilopochtli yo le doy mis flores" song lyric from "Ni Huitzilopochtli Cuicatl" learned in Aztec dance circles.

Healing Wild Woman

Andariega has become a rallying cry toward reclamation and movement by way of the work of my colegas Andariegas as inspired by our studies of Tey Diana Rebolledo's *Women Singing in the Snow: A cultural analysis of Chicana literature.* University of Arizona Press, 1995.

Al Hocico Libre

First performed on stage with El Teatro Campesino's *Palabra Vol. Solo 2021* show and later published in *Xinacthli Journal— Journal X* in their Spring 2022 issue.

De puro corazón reference inspired by the poetic legacy of José Antonio Burciaga as expressed in "Lo del corazón" in *Undocumented Love: Amor Indocumentado: A Personal Anthology of Poetry.* San José, CA: Chusma House Publications. 1992.

Chiasmus

Inspired by the 2008 National Associaton of Chicana and Chicano Studies Annual Conference where Alicia Gaspar de Alba and Alma López presented on the work of Alma López. During the presentation, Gaspar de Alba introduced chiasmus as a trope of repetition and reversal where the reversal and disruption of the previously expressed version offer a different way of seeing the work/world. Also see:

Gaspar de Alba, Alicia and Alma López, editors. *Our Lady of Controversy: Alma López's "Irreverent Apparition".* University of Texas Press, 2011. pp. 114-115.

All Ironies Intended

"Retrofitted memories" inspired by the work and scholarship of Maylei Blackwell as expressed in *¡Chicana Power!: Contested Histories of Feminism in the Chicano Movement.* University of Texas Press, 2011.

Rosie's Revenge

A response, in part, to Rodolfy "Corky" Gonzales' 1967 epic poem "I Am Joaquin."

"All the world's a stage" is a reference taken from William Shakespeare's pastoral comedy *As You Like It,* that invokes the drama stage days of my high school years. The phrase also invokes the processes of signification and Chela Sandoval's "oppositional consciousness."

ibid

"ibid" is itself an abbreviation from ibidem, meaning "in the same place" and used in citations to quickly cite a source that has already been cited in full, in a previous footnote or endnote, directing the reader to the previous citation. Here, it is also used to unpack some of the tensions articulated in the poem "Rosie's Revenge" to make a point about circling back to revise as we find ourselves in the same place, still in excavation, unearthing and revisiting knowledge while grappling with multi-layered erasure.

Beautiful Soul Speak

Inspired by a beautiful celebration of community, organized in response to controversy surrounding Cinco de Mayo in the small town of Morgan Hill, California.

Orenda

According to the Haudenosaunee, we experience different things, learning and comprehending more as we tap into our spiritual power, developing our sense of self in relation to the well-being of others within the bigger collective power of nature's energies.

And Still, We Braid

Have you ever noticed the only thing separating rest and resist is "si." Imagine, what if.

Check stand 5 is a line inspired by the poetry of fellow poet and danzante, Salvador Hernandez.

Gente Decente

First shared at the Farmworker Caravan at Emma Prusch Farm Park in San José, California in 2021.

Chinga Tu Afterthought

First shared on stage at the 2019 San José Women's March in San José, California.

En Protesta

"Sí, se puede" inspired by the motto of the United Farm Workers of America, originated by activist Dolores Huerta.

Tortilla Consciousness

Written to honor the teen students during my short time teaching high school. The line "peel my love like an onion" is a reference to the work of Ana Castillo who was a huge part of my literary journey of self-excavation as a young adult.

Contentious

"This bridge called my back" is, in part, a tribute to the work of the same name - *This Bridge Called My Back: Writings by Radical Women of Color,* a feminist anthology edited by Cherríe Moraga and Gloria Anzaldúa.

Drum Speak

I was first introduced to the Four Agreements by way of youth development work at the Mexican American Community Services Agency (MACSA) in San José, California, where we also referenced the work of Don Miguel Ruiz who elaborates on the knowledge of the four agreements as a practical guide to personal freedom in his book *The Four Agreements.* Based on Toltec wisdoms, the four agreements - as a practice of personal accountability toward collective relationality - is also present in Aztec danza circles.

Control-Alt-Delete

"The Payless Mural" is more accurately named el "Mural de la Raza" and adorned the Payless Shoe Store wall of my youth on Story Road in San José for a span of over three decades. Created by artist Jose Meza Velasquez in 1985 with the help of local youth, the mural depicted highlights of Chicana/o/x history. It always gave me a dose of possibility and historical magic, alongside the newly acquired kicks/shoes. The mural was shadily painted over in 2018, without public comment, in spite of efforts to restore the work. In the dark of night, the white-washing of a multi-layered history remains tragically symbolic of dynamics of hostile erasure that extend beyond the mural itself.

I Dream

First shared at the Santa Clara County 29th Annual Domestic Violence Conference in October of 2022.

The theme of remembrance and re-membering is inspired by so many pieces of knowledge and experience. Yet, this particular set of lines - "The ancestors -they say we don't have to struggle to learn; It's about how we learn to remember" - is inspired by the words and work of Native activist and poet John Trudell in his "Listening/Honor Song" track of *Tribal Voice:*

> "you must remember the gentleness of time
> you are struggling to be who you are
> you say you want to learn the old ways
> struggling to learn
> when all you must do is remember ... "

Mujeres de Posteridad

"Wicked ways" is a direct reference to the poetry collection of Sandra Cisneros' *My Wicked Ways* and extends beyond the work to call in the moments of shared conversation with comadres throughout the years.

"Nepantla" invokes the work of Gloria E. Anzaldúa as a starting point for exploring the Nahuatl concept for the in-between space between two worlds, while also calling in the collective excavation of the nepantla state beyond what was articulated in the original publication of *Borderlands/La Frontera* in 1987.

Un-Preyed

A portion of this poem appears as a series of lines in "Al Hocico Libre." In trying to recall which came first, I honestly cannot say; which is worth mentioning because poems have their own way about non-linear time lines, along with their corresponding braided ripples and such.

Inked Drawings Throughout

Throughout my life, I have kept notebooks of writing mixed with drawings. In recent years, I've paid more attention to how the drawings and words are in constant conversation with each other. In the past decade, I have also developed a preference for black ink drawings that I later connected to *in tlilli tlapalli*. The influence of some of my favorite Chicana/o/x artists and our shared defiance of mainstream conventions of what qualifies art as such is also strikingly present.

Years back, I began more intentionally pairing poems and artwork to share for National Poetry Month. I also recall hastily displaying a series of those works alongside each other for an arts space open studio event and found it affirming that folks kept asking when and where they could purchase that collection.

Somewhere in that journey, someone likened the stylistic choice to Shel Silverstein, which I suppose is not untrue given how much I've always loved his poetry - both as a child and as an adult; and still, that description is not quite accurate in intentionality.

Later, I saw the work of poet Gris Muñoz find its way into the world in *Coatlicue Girl,* and as I turned the pages appreciating the black and white drawings, I felt affirmed. In putting this collection together and tracing the influence of other poets on my work, I was also delighted to see that the work of the late José Antonio Burciaga in *Undocumented Love* did the same.

Cover Design

During the span of years that it took for this collection to come into formation, life things have continued to happen. In that span of time, my family has grown, I have ebbed and flowed between highs and lows, we've survived and thrived, grieved and loved, fought and celebrated as gente, and my tres guerreras have taught me so much about remembering.

As I was struggling with the cover design, I knew I wanted something that represented both the simple and complicated parts of this journey of remembrance, reclamation, and recovery. I knew I wanted the cover to be vibrant, culturally signifying, and slightly mysterious. The constants were braids and weaving.

Knowing that I have always had a desire to design textiles, I knew there would be some element of "pattern design" or "surface design" incorporated as well. I had already proven that tendency as part of my "repertoire" when I released my coloring books a few years back. Somewhere in all of that, the work of Anna Alvarado, a Latinx creator and storyteller, popped up on my social media feed. Immediately, I felt affirmed in my choice and I am grateful for the inadvertent permisos the fellow artist helped me locate in embracing the power of a faceless portrait of sorts - simply by being in existence.

Then, as I glanced up while typing these words, I realized that the same can be said of the artwork hanging in so many of our casitas, such as Diego Rivera's "Vendedora de Flores".

I draw my children often and also dabble in self-portraits that represent different facets of me. In attempting to capture some version of myself within danza, simultaneously stepping into the past and the future as represented by the floral embroidery kept alive through indigenous weaving and encaje, I subconsciously ended up with a drawing of what looks so much like my youngest guerrera embarking on a journey of cultural wonder, rooted in love, embraced by the rebozos of so many of our grandmothers:

the little girl waiting past the longing
-- embraced by so much belonging.

Turns out she is all of us.

Rosanna Alvarez is a multi-faceted interdisciplinary story-teller, artist, and poet. She describes her writing as a constant process of excavation and of re-membering herself whole while translating the living legacy of the stories that have shaped us into who we have become both individually and collectively. She is a boot wearing, tejana loving Chicana, a mother of three guerreras, and a trucker's wife.

Her work has been published in *Label Me Latina/o, Journal X, Modern Latina Magazine, Chicana/Latina Studies: The Journal of Mujeres Activas en Letras y Cambio Social, St. Sucia Zine,* and *Eastside Magazine San José.* She will be a featured contributor in the forthcoming compilation of La Raza Historical Society of Santa Clara Valley's *21st Century Reflections on the Early Writings of Luis Miguel Valdez.*

OTHER WORKS:

- *Guerrera: A Coloring Book for Warriors Everywhere*
- *Hechicera: A Coloring Book for Chingonas Everywhere*
- *Dreams, Serendipity and Wisdom: A Coloring Book Meditation*

Made in the USA
Middletown, DE
26 August 2024

59273265R00097